## A SURVIVAL GUIDE

# SHED OR YOU'RE DEAD®

**KEEP** GROWTH. CHANGE. POSSIBILITIES. **SHEDDING!** ™ INC.

**Tina Altman**
VP of Client Solutions
612-298-2622
Tina@KeepShedding.com

877-5-SHED-NOW
www.KeepShedding.com

**Kathy B. Dempsey**
*Award Winning Author, Keynote Speaker, Change Expert*

## A SURVIVAL GUIDE

# SHED OR YOU'RE DEAD®

## A FAST ACTING CHANGE Rx FOR HEALTHCARE PROFESSIONALS

KATHY B. DEMPSEY

Trey Press
Phoenix, Arizona

# A Survival Guide
# Shed or You're Dead®
## A fast acting change Rx for
## healthcare professionals

Kathy B. Dempsey

Published by:
Trey Press
Phoenix, Arizona

Artwork: Joe Kulka
Cover layout: Singles Design

Printed in the United States of America

ISBN: 978-0-9742926-9-4

Dedicated to John McCallie Bolinger, MD, (1949-2005)
who faithfully dedicated his life to the field of psychiatry –
to helping people SHED. His boundless good cheer and
unshakable belief in a world that holds hope for everyone
inspired many to climb up to unimaginable heights.
His infectious laugh, loving heart, and generous spirit lives
on in the multitude of lives he touched.

# Table of Contents

Preface: Why Don't All Doctors Ask You This? ...............1

Diagnosis: People Don't Know How to SHED! ...............9

    The #1 Skill We're Hiring For... ..............10

    The SHED Pill ..............12

Shedding 101 ..............15

    The Shedding Philosophy ..............16

    The Process of Shedding ..............19

    Rapid Shedding: The Antidote for the
    Change Crisis ..............21

    The Five Laws of Shedding ..............22

    Your First Shedding Experience ..............23

    Three R's of Shedding ..............26

SHED Attachments ..............31

    Shedding Primary Attachments ..............32

    Shedding Mental Models ..............34

    Shedding Expectations ..............38

SHED Resistance ..............41

    The Pain of Shedding ..............42

    Celebration Accelerates Shedding ..............46

    Overcoming Fear: The Biggest Barrier
    to Shedding ..............49

    Why People Resist Change and Refuse to SHED ...51

SHED Management ..............55

    Awareness Management ..............56

    Energy Management ..............58

Control Management.................................................66

Personal Shedding...................................................70

To SHED or Not to SHED? ......................................71

Avoiding the Three Deadly Syndromes.................72

SHED Styles™...............................................................77

Development of SHED Styles...............................78

Understanding Your SHED Style..........................79

Adapting Your SHED Style to Achieve
Positive Results......................................................82

How to Lead a More Efficient Team.......................88

SHED Leadership............................................................91

How to Help Other People SHED.........................92

7 New Skills Every Healthcare Worker Needs.......95

Who Killed Communication?.................................97

35 Strategies to Keep Communication Alive.........102

Ready, Set, SHED! ........................................................105

Avoiding Premature Death.....................................106

Lenny's Favorite Quotes to SHED for Success™...108

SHED for Success™ Rx Reminders.........................110

Your SHED Page.....................................................111

Your Personal SHED Rx Action Plan.....................112

Acknowledgments...........................................................113

About Kathy B. Dempsey................................................114

About Lenny T. Lizard.....................................................116

Need Support to Help You SHED?..................................118

Need a System to SHED for Success? .............................119

# Preface:
# Why Don't All Doctors Ask You This?

How many times do you need to hear something before you listen? For me, it's a lot. My mother told me I was strong-willed (a.k.a. stubborn).

In 2007, several colleagues strongly recommended I read the book *Eat, Pray, Love*. I kept dismissing their nudges saying I didn't have time for pleasure reading. Months later on the way to Europe to speak, a whisper turned into a shout. The book stared me in the face at JFK airport. I finally bought it and promised myself I'd read it on the plane.

Why was this book significant to me? The author, Elizabeth Gilbert, shares her adventurous journey of self-discovery as she travels through Italy, Bali and India. While reading the book, it hit me: I'd been to Italy. I'd been to Bali. I just needed to get to India! It seemed like a sign...

The next day while sitting in an Internet café in Switzerland, I received another "sign" from the universe; an email arrived from a colleague about going to India. I booked the trip immediately.

Unfortunately, within 24 hours of arriving in India, I became deathly sick. After dragging my body around for a few days, I finally decided to see a medical doctor.

I arrived at the appointment and was escorted into the doctor's office. A kind, middle-aged, male doctor walked in. The first thing he said was, "Tell me about your typical day?" Startled by his response, I said, "Excuse me? What did you just say?" He repeated the question:

### *Tell me about your typical day?*

So I told him. "I get up at 5 a.m., jump in the shower, dress quickly, finish packing my suitcase, rush out the door and head for the airport. I arrive at the airport in time to grab a bite to eat in the fast food court. I check email on my phone before the flight attendant insists that I shut it off. US Airways seat 4B turns into my virtual office for the day. My connecting flight is delayed so I sit on the floor at O'Hare International Airport for two hours.

Finally, we board the plane for the next flight. I arrive at my hotel late at night and collapse into bed. I try to get 5-6 hours of sleep before I have to get up and speak. Then I do it all over again."

### The Doctor's Response:
After hearing about my typical day, the doctor said. "You can heal yourself. I'm just here to give you a few suggestions, to guide you. What you decide to do is really up to you."

Here's what the doctor recommended:
- Establish some routines
- Get eight hours sleep every night
- Drink more water
- Exercise daily
- Eat healthier, smaller, more frequent meals
- Avoid spicy food

I walked out of his office stunned. I had *never* experienced anything like this. Where was my prescription? My lab tests? My CT scan? He didn't even take my blood pressure! What if something was really wrong? What if I caught some dreaded disease?

I was irritated. I knew all that stuff! Didn't he know I was a healthcare professional? His treatment plan seemed like something he'd dusted off from an elementary school health class.

But as I reflected on the visit later that night, I had to shed my denial and realize he was right. There were so many things I could do to take better care of myself.

Even though I had been in healthcare for over 30 years, I had established deeply rooted patterns of working long hours and had fallen into unhealthy lifestyle habits that dated back to my early career as a healthcare professional.

I not only went the extra mile at work, I went the extra *ten* miles. When someone called in sick, I seemed to be the first one to agree to work a double shift. That's what I was taught a good healthcare professional did. I was rewarded for my dedication. In fact, I was promoted to be a hospital administrator where I consistently worked 12 hours a day.

The Indian doctor didn't give me the formal diagnosis I expected. But if he *had* given me one with regards to my own "healthcare" habits, I realize now that it would have been: ***You didn't SHED!***

After traveling all around the world on my *Eat, Pray, Love* journey, it all came down to one simple lesson: SHED, SHED, SHED!

I finally admitted the doctor was right. His recommendations were just the impetus that I needed. A few months after my trip to India, I decided to SHED and make major changes to my own *"healthcare."* I decided to reclaim control of my life. I moved from the Philadelphia area to Scottsdale, Arizona. I sold my house, got rid of 95% of everything I owned, packed a few boxes and headed West. (OK, did I forget to say my partner, Lenny the Lizard, had been pleading me with me for years to relocate to Arizona to be closer to his relatives? Confused about Lenny? Turn to page 116 and read his bio.)

**Why Did I Write This Book?**
Our healthcare system is facing its most challenging time ever. The system is broken because it's based on a faulty model of "you break down and we fix it." Costs are skyrocketing. Internal resources and work capacity are being enormously tested. Healthcare is consuming 16% of our GDP. And questions about right to healthcare, access, fairness, efficiency, cost, choice, value, and quality are being hotly debated.

Healthcare professionals must prepare to deal with the increasing workplace demands.

Adding to the healthcare challenge is the fact that unhealthy lifestyle habits are killing us. Nearly 40% of all deaths in the United States every year are a result of smoking, poor diet, lack of exercise or alcohol abuse.

As individuals, most healthcare professionals don't have much control over healthcare reform legislation or how other people choose to live their lives. But we do have control over these two things:

1. **Personally:** Taking better care of ourselves.

2. **Professionally**: Equipping ourselves with the skills and motivation to more effectively manage rapid healthcare change.

I'll explore point #2, professional shedding, in depth throughout the rest of the book. But first, let's look at what we can each do personally.

**What You Can Do Personally**
If we were honest with ourselves, many of us would admit that once we began our healthcare career, the daily stresses of delivering care began to override the core intent of our own health. The tacit message to the public has become, "Do as I say, not as I do." We have to do something different to stay healthy and prepare ourselves to deal with the upcoming changes. Healthcare professionals must SHED!

**It's Not Just About Knowledge, It's About Action!**
Ironically, healthcare professionals have more knowledge about staying healthy than any other profession. We counsel our patients about it every day.

And yet, heart disease, cancer and diabetes all top the list of killers. But it's not just about knowledge. If being healthy was just about knowledge, we wouldn't have any doctors who smoked, nurses who are overweight or healthcare workers that didn't start their day with exercise.

Just think about how our industry could be positively impacted if we, as healthcare professionals, started taking care of ourselves. We certainly would put a dent in the Surgeon General's statistic: Seven out of ten illnesses are lifestyle related.

If *we* don't set the example for the public, who will? If *we* don't stand up and make our own healthcare important and embrace the foundational principles upon which our profession is based, the disease called *"Didn't SHED"* will quickly rise to the top of the "Causes of Death For Healthcare Workers" list.

## *Are You Ready to SHED?*

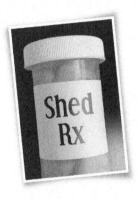

Take care of your body. Where else are you going to live?

# DIAGNOSIS:
# People Don't Know
# How to SHED!

# The #1 Skill We're Hiring For Is . . .

Recently, I was speaking at a major healthcare conference. Before I was introduced, the vice president of the 10,000 employee system stood up and announced,

*"The number one skill we are hiring for today is the ability to learn on the fly!"*

Ten years ago that statement would have been unthinkable. Back then, people asked: Where did you go to school? What's your work history? Can you take a blood pressure reading? Not the "ability to learn on the fly."

In reality, what the hospital executive was saying is the ability to adapt quickly to change is paramount. The new expectation is: "What we're hiring you for today is probably *not* what we are going to be asking you to do tomorrow."

*No Organization Can Thrive Unless their People Can SHED!*

Why do 75% of all change efforts fail? They fail largely because people feel left out of the process and lack the knowledge, skills and motivation to adapt to the organization's new systems, processes and procedures.

Successful healthcare professionals will embody "temporary" as the norm and learn to promptly detach from ineffective roles, ideas and "the way we have always done it."

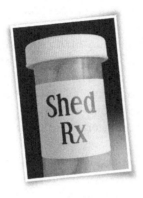

# Embody temporary
as the norm.

# The SHED Pill

Imagine you could administer a pill — the SHED Pill — to everyone you worked with and, as soon as you gave it to them, they would accept change faster.

After taking the SHED Pill, your team would have the skills and motivation to navigate all the turbulent changes going on in the healthcare industry. No negative attitudes. No resistance to change. They could immediately learn on the fly. In short, after taking the SHED Pill they would instantaneously be transformed into "Super-shedders":

What would your organization be like if everyone was a Super-shedder? The results might be:

- Increased productivity
- Improved bottom line
- Healthier and happier employees

I must caution you… since the "SHED Pill" is still in clinical trials, and hasn't been approved by the FDA, we will need to equip ourselves and others with the necessary skills and sustainable motivation to lead and master change on our own.

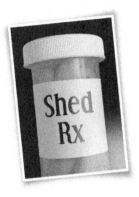

# Commit to being a
# Super-shedder!

# SHEDDING 101

# The Philosophy of Shedding

The philosophy of shedding was birthed on July 29, 1998 at Memorial Hospital in Chattanooga, Tennessee.

It was 7 a.m. and time for our quarterly ethics committee meeting at the hospital. I rushed in and at the last minute ran into a colleague, David Mann, who I hadn't seen in a while. Here's how our conversation went:

"Good morning, David. How are you?"

"I'm fine, Kathy, but my lizard is dead."

Startled, yet intrigued, I said, "Your lizard is dead? What happened?"

"He didn't shed his skin...and if lizards don't shed their skin, they die," said David.

"Why?" I asked.

He explained. "Lizards grow by shedding their skin. If they don't shed, they aren't growing and they die."

I reflected on that for a moment and then replied, "David, what can we, as humans, learn from the lizard?"

"We as humans grow physically, mentally, and spiritually... and if we don't grow we die," he said.

"So what does our old skin represent? Old habits? Negative attitudes? Unhealthy relationships?" I asked.

Then, at the very same time, we looked at each other and the light bulb went on for both of us. "Shed or you're dead!"

Two transformational things happened that day. First, it gave me a benchmark for my personal growth path. Second, I had a metaphor, "Shed or You're Dead," featuring Lenny the Lizard, who become my life-long companion, alter-ego, business partner and vehicle for helping people SHED!

Remarkably, lizards can teach us a lot about growth and change. One key lesson for healthcare professionals and organizations is that if they don't shed, they become unhealthy and die!

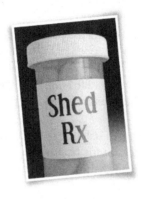

# It's 100% Your Choice:
# Shed or You're Dead®!

# The Process of Shedding

**Shedding is a two-part process.**

1. **Letting go of the old.** "The old" represents all those things that are unhealthy and are no longer serving you. They may have once served you, but they no longer do now.

   Did you ever use a typewriter? Do you use one now? Why not? It no longer serves you – you use a computer instead. A typewriter was a necessity 20 years ago, now it's an obsolete device.

2. **Taking on the new.** The second part of shedding is taking on all the new skills, knowledge and healthy habits that will help you continue to grow.

**The Continuous Cycle of Shedding**

Taking on          Letting go
the new            of the old

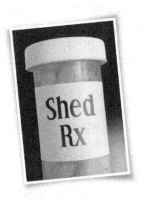

Routinely ask
yourself, what no
longer serves me?

# Rapid Shedding:
# The Antidote for the Change Crisis

We are going through unprecedented change. It is at a crisis level and there is no sign of relief. In fact, some experts say you will go through more change this year than your grandparents did in their entire lifetime!

Change is even changing. In the past, change was episodic. There were periods of intense change followed by periods of less intense change. It ebbed and flowed more like the natural tides coming in and out on the beach each day. Today, change is continuous. It is like a relentless tidal wave that never lets up.

**The Change Crisis:**
**How change is changing**

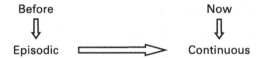

It's not surprising that change is the biggest catalyst for shedding. It is demanding we change faster than ever before. Rapid shedding skills are the antidote needed to counteract the change crisis. The quicker we embrace these skills the better prepared we will be to face the ever accelerating pace of continuous change.

Buckle your seatbelts! It's a crisis that is here to stay.

# The Five Laws of Shedding

1. **Shedding is a natural part of growth.** Humans tend to make the process much more painful than it needs to be.

2. **Shedding is about loss and gain.** It's a cycle. To gain something you must let go of something else first.

3. **Shedding offers the greatest opportunity for growth.** Change doesn't equal growth; it just offers the opportunity to grow if we allow it.

4. **Shedding is a choice.** Every decision that we make has a consequence. Resistance to change can be costly.

5. **Shedding is nurtured within a support environment.** People, animals and even plants all grow best when surrounded by a nurturing environment.

# Your First Shedding Experience

The basis of shedding, or change, is rooted in two of life's core necessities:

Attachment
and
Detachment

Do you remember being born? If not, take your hand and feel that button in the middle of your stomach. It's evidence you were born!

Imagine you are back in your mom's womb. It was warm and secure. You didn't have to worry about paying the rent or mortgage. You had a nine month rent free lease!

You didn't have to worry about going to the grocery store or the kids yelling, "Mom, what are we going to have for dinner?" You had 24/7 infusion of nutrition.

You didn't have to worry about bills, or bosses, or teenagers, or patients. Life was good!

What happened nine months later? You were evicted! Mom decided to downsize! Fetal foreclosure! Then what did somebody do with a pair of scissors? They cut the cord. And what did most of us do? We cried! And if we could have spoken at that time what would we have said? "Put me back in!"

From the day you are born until the day you die, you will continue to go through a series of attachments and detachments. Not the physical ones like being attached to Mom by a cord, but emotional ones.

Your ability to deal with life's detachments is critical for your professional success and happiness.

The primary focus of attachments at birth (our cord) and death (our bodies) are physical. However, the primary focus of attachments throughout the rest of our lives are *emotional*.

### Primary Focus of Attachments

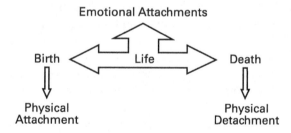

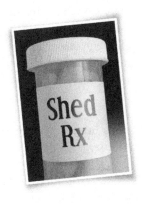

Learning to navigate
life's attachments and
detachments is critical
to your success
and happiness.

# Three R's of Shedding

1. **Release the attachment.**
   Attachment brings to mind a safe and secure environment. Just as you were attached to your mom with a cord for nine months and it nurtured your growth, the womb eventually no longer served you. You were in rapid shedding mode. Nature knew this and literally forced your mom to "downsize" and to release the attachment.

   Attachments are only healthy for a period of time, then they must be released.

   ***Goal:*** *Identify your emotional attachments and release them quickly.*

2. **Reframe the situation.**
   Some changes may initially appear overwhelmingly negative, but with time most people recognize change is necessary or it's a blessing in disguise. Reframing — viewing a situation from a different perspective or a more positive light — is an essential skill. Successful people quickly see the positive side of change and don't allow a situation, no matter how bad, to get them stuck or derailed. Instead of it taking five years to get over a loss, maybe it only takes five months, five weeks, five days, five minutes or even five seconds.

   Can you imagine what you were thinking when someone cut your cord? Talk about having a bad day!

You might have been thinking: "Life is over! Where am I going to live? What am I going to eat?" Now years later you have been able to reframe the situation. You realize that the detachment gave you life. In reality, change – or the apparent loss – created space for something new to emerge.

*Goal: Develop a short reframe quotient by shedding negativity quickly and looking at change from the most positive light.*

3. **Refocus your energy.**

Eckert Tolle, author of *The Power of Now*, claims that 93% of our thoughts are repetitive and useless. He asserts that most people are not fully present. They are either obsessing about the past or worried about the future. Think about how much more energy could be harnessed if you were fully present and focused. When distracted or overwhelmed, employ your most powerful innate skill acquired at birth – a deep cleansing breath. It will immediately refocus, reenergize and bring you back to the now. Consider using your belly button as a "trigger" to refocus. Physically touching it will help you center.

*Goal: Stay fully present and focused on what actions are needed to move forward.*

## The Cycle of the 3 R's of Shedding

Refocus your energy

Release the attachment

Reframe the situation

You can use the three R's of shedding for any challenging situation at work or in life. Practice them and they will become as easy and natural as riding a bike. Here is an example:

---

***Challenging situation:***
*You get a flat tire on the way to work.*

---

1. **Release the attachment:**
   What do you need to detach from?
   *You are not going to be to work on time for your 8 a.m. meeting.*

2. **Reframe the situation:**
   How can I view this situation from the most positive light?
   *No one was in an accident. I am safe. I'm glad a have a cell phone.*

3. **Refocus your energy:**
   What action will I take to move forward?
   *Call work, tell them I will be late. Call AAA to come help me.*

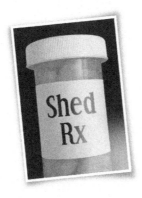

# Practice the 3 R's of Shedding

1. Release the attachment
2. Reframe the situation
3. Refocus your energy

# SHEDDING
# ATTACHMENTS

# Shedding Primary Attachments

There are three primary attachments that are most difficult for humans to shed.

**Types of Attachments**

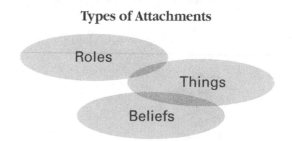

1. **Roles**

   We get attached to our roles and we often over identify ourselves by those roles. For instance, I am a nurse, a manager, an executive, or a spouse. We will play some role, significant or insignificant, with every person we meet. It is alright to have these roles, but realize that all roles are temporary and will end one day.

2. **Things**

   Humans get attached to *stuff*. *My* house, *my* parking space, *my* shift, *my* pen! Anytime "my" is used, it is a signal of attachment to something.

3. **Beliefs**

   Beliefs are our way of thinking about things – the way "it" should be, traditions or the "good old days." That's the way we have always done it. *I like paper charting!*

CAUTION: Role losses, like losing a job, trigger reactions in all three areas. People often spiral down quickly as they experience compounding losses – the role, the things the role provided for them financially and a shattering of their beliefs. *People told me if I became a nurse, I would always have a job!*

# Shedding Mental Models

Our mental models, or our perception of the world around us, affect how we are going to respond to change.

For example, let's say that you remind me of my sister. Well, I hate my sister! (I don't actually hate my sister, I love her.) But if I *did* hate my sister and you reminded me of my sister, how do you think I would respond to you every time I saw you? Probably not well.

Our mental models are the instantaneous ways we filter, or judge, everything that comes through our brain. Most of us are not really conscious of our mental models. Based on our past experiences and frames of reference, we either filter information with "Oh No!" or "Wahoo!"

Quickly read the list of changes below. Imagine that the list of the changes is actually happening to you. Would your mental model be "Oh No!" or "Wahoo!"?

- You are transferred to new job in Fargo, North Dakota
- You are transferred to new job in Maui, Hawaii.
- You now have your boss' job and responsibilities.
- You now have your boss' salary.
- The kids are moving out of the house.
- The kids are moving back in the house.
- JCAHO survey team is coming today.
- You are going to have a baby!

If you want to change, change your mental models first.

The faster you switch from "Oh no!" to "Wahoo!" the faster you can transform your life.

---

## "Oh No" JCAHO Case Study

**Situation:** For almost 30 years, I've observed a vicious "Oh No!" JCAHO cycle everywhere I've worked. Every three years right before JCAHO arrived, staff would become stressed out and patient care suffered.

I met with the CEO of our healthcare system to discuss this issue. We were doing some incredible things, so why couldn't we get excited that the JCAHO surveyors were coming?

**Strategy:** I suggested a *"Back to the Future"* theme for our performance improvement presentation. The time machine would show where we had been, where we were and where we were going with performance improvement. I suggested he dress up like the crazy professor and greet the surveyors at the door.

The CEO agreed to go along with the crazy idea on one condition: I had to get everyone excited.

I gathered 20 staff from front line employees to the executive office. Instead of a boring board room presentation, the performance improvement presentation was given in a huge community room. We rented a smoke machine and strobe light. We covered all the tables in aluminum foil. I went to surgery and got a white jump suit, proceeded to nuclear medicine and picked up a radioactive sign and ended up in the CEO's office to dress him up.

In fact, everyone got dressed up and involved: RN's, respiratory therapist, patients, even cardiac surgeons. Staff were so excited; they couldn't wait for the surveyors to come. We all stood at the door and greeted the surveyors.

**Results:** After our presentation, the surveyors gave us a standing ovation. Then they stood and said, "Survey over one day early!" We received 100% on our performance improvement presentation.

Not only that, we became one of the top 100 hospitals in the country, number one in customer satisfaction across the nation with our system, and we exceeded our budgetary goal of $5,000,000!

**The secret:** Who would have thought my crazy idea would work? It all came down to changing mental models. And look at the results when 4,000 people transformed their JCAHO mental model from "Oh No!" to "Wahoo!"

---

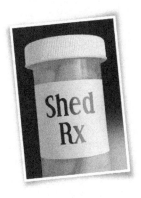

# If you want to change, change your mental models first!

# Shedding Expectations

In 2005, I volunteered to spend a month in Africa taking care of orphans who had lost their parents to AIDS. I was overwhelmed to discover there were over 12,000 orphans just in the small city of Ndola, Zambia. During an afternoon visit with the local bishop, I inquired about how the orphans could be so happy, so full of joy while they had nothing?

"They *have* no expectations," he replied.

"They have no expectation of getting an education, no expectation of having parents and no expectation of having a home."

We all have our reference points. To the African AIDS orphans, our shrinking 401K statements the last couple years would be like winning the lottery!

A survey cited in *Psychology Today* revealed Americans are becoming more depressed than ever before. Researchers believe the phenomenon is closely linked to the unrealistic expectations of the American Dream. The more people focus on a materialistic pathway to happiness, the less happy they tend to be.

Now, there is nothing wrong with having expectations. Expectations can propel us to dream, set goals and accomplish things in life. Unnecessary pain and suffering arises when we *overattach* to our expectations. Learning to realistically revisit and adjust them appropriately will enhance your ability to SHED.

CAUTION: Expectations can be spoken or unspoken. Our expectations, shaped by our current reality and past experiences, greatly influence our ability to adapt to change.

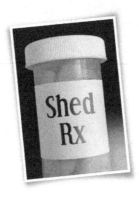

# Revisit and adjust your expectations.

# SHED
# RESISTANCE

# The Pain of Shedding

Why is shedding so painful? The reality is shedding — or change — is a loss of some kind. We believe we are losing something of value.

So whether it is getting a job or losing a job, getting sick or getting well, getting married or getting divorced, financial gain or financial loss, life is about shedding. And shedding is about letting go of the loss in order to gain something new.

It doesn't matter whether you work at a health care organization that has ten employees or 10,000 employees, when it comes down to organizational change, it all comes down to what is the *personal* loss that each of us is experiencing. The more intense the personal loss, the greater degree of attachment.

**Shedding Intensity**

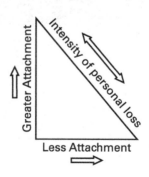

CAUTION: When someone appears to overreact to a change, it's usually an indication of a greater personal loss and emotional attachment.

To move forward, the loss must be dealt with and it must be grieved.

Below are the four **LADA Stages of Change** that most of us experience at some level when we shed.

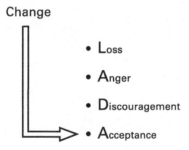

These stages are fluid and don't always follow each other sequentially. In a perfect world, whenever we experienced change, we would immediately leap to acceptance. Unfortunately, we are human and for most of us it takes a bit longer.

The goal is to acknowledge your feelings and don't get stuck. Keep Shedding!

This summary of the LADA stages of change shows you how people think, feel and behave in each stage.

Suggestions are given for each stage: What question can be asked and what helps people move through the stages more successfully.

## LADA Stages of Change

| Stage | Think | Feel | Behavior | Ask? | What helps? |
|---|---|---|---|---|---|
| Loss | No, not me! | Numb, fearful | Paralyzed, denial | What's the worst thing that could happen? | Acknowledge fears and emotions |
| Anger | Why me? | Anger, resentment | Resistance, bargaining | What information can I obtain? | Information, plan with options |
| Discouragement | Poor me… | Sad, overwhelmed | Unproductive, withdrawn | Can I hold on to the belief that the current challenge is creating space for something new to emerge? | Stay focused, prioritize, manage personal energy, explore possibilities |
| Acceptance | Ok me! | Content, re-energized | Productive, helpful | What is the best thing that could happen? | Ask, share and integrate lessons learned |

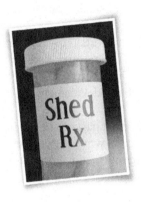

When change occurs,
acknowledge the loss
and move towards
acceptance.

# Celebration Accelerates Shedding

Just as loss is part of shedding, so is celebration. Do you realize you celebrate the most painful day of your life — your birthday — every single year? Why?

Celebration is a healthy ritual that accelerates shedding. It marks the end of one thing and the beginning of something else. When you celebrate you are actually acknowledging a loss, a detachment.

Rituals are an important part of helping people cope with life's transitions. That's why every society known to man has rites of passage, a ritual event that marks a person's progress from one place to another.

The dictionary defines a ritual as: *An act or series of acts carried out to relieve anxiety or to forestall the development of anxiety.*

Most humans' anxiety levels heighten when change occurs. We need something to help us move through the change.

Don't underestimate the power of celebratory rituals. It may seem like fluff, but it is an essential component of facilitating healthy change. It's well worth investing the time and effort to celebrate.

William Bridges, author of *Managing Transitions*, says when people are experiencing change and loss, they find comfort in something tangible that they can hold on to.

If you are involved in organizational change, consider giving people a physical reminder that represents what they are shedding. It can be a small gift, a certificate or a memento. Whether it is serious or light, people's anxiety will be diminished when they can anchor the change with something they can touch and feel.

When the demands of change intensify, resist the urge to postpone or cancel celebratory rituals. They're important and shouldn't be forgotten.

If you truly want to accelerate the shedding process, think about celebrating in advance. I have worked with many organizations over the years to facilitate shedding celebrations.

We threw a party and celebrated the future success prior to it actually occurring. It's like programming your unconscious for super-shedding. The results are mind-boggling!

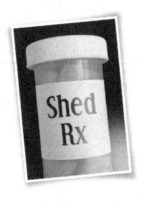

SHEDebrate!
The more change,
the more you need to
celebrate!

# Overcoming Fear:
# The Biggest Barrier to Shedding

## F E A R !

A staggering 95% of people say that fear is the number one thing that holds them back at work and in life.

A few years ago, I had the privilege of speaking for The Disney Corporation in Orlando. After experiencing an incredible backstage tour, I was surprised to discover that Walt Disney was afraid of mice.

So what did he do? He embraced his biggest fear and transformed it into his biggest professional success. He chose to make his fear less scary. He added big ears and a fun playful face and named his fear Mickey.

When you resist facing your fear, there is usually a price to pay — not only to you, but also to others as well.

If Walt Disney had never faced his fear, there would be no Disney World. Can you imagine the millions of people being robbed of their happy childhood memories and family vacations?

Embrace your fears. Make them your friend.

The cure for fear is ACTION.

Fear + Action = Courage

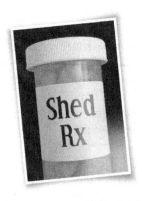

# Courageously
# embrace your fear
# and take action!

# Why People Resist Change and Refuse to SHED

It is a natural human reaction to resist change, especially when we don't initiate it. Here are the top reasons why people resist change and refuse to SHED and simple ways to help them start the shedding process.

- **I don't need to change.**
  People have a natural tendency towards maintaining the status quo and their comfort zone.

  *Help: Give them information and clearly explain why the change is needed and the benefits to them and the organization.*

- **I don't have the skills and abilities required.**
  People know how to operate in the existing order, but fear they might not have the capabilities that will be required of them with the change.

  *Help: Have them identify all their current skills. Encourage them to continue to learn new skills so they will be prepared for future changes.*

- **You won't need me anymore.**
  People fear the unknown and change implies uncertainty, which often heightens anxiety.

  *Help: Remind them that all job roles are temporary. If their job ends, help them with the transition.*

- **I can't keep up.**
  People find it difficult to cope with either the level or pace of the change.

  *Help: Encourage them to prioritize tasks and learn to manage their personal energy.*

- **I don't agree with the change.**
  People may feel that the change is heading in a wrong direction, doesn't make sense or isn't relevant.

  *Help: Invite this person to express his or her thoughts and feelings.*

- **I am losing something of value.**
  People resist change because they believe they are losing something of value, whether it's real or perceived.

  *Help: Urge them to focus their energy on what they will gain — not lose.*

- **I am sure this will eventually go away if I just wait it out. (Peter Pan Syndrome)**
  People have magical thinking or false beliefs and often fool themselves into believing everything will be just fine and magically go back to the way it was. This is often called the "Peter Pan Syndrome."

  *Help: Work with them to avoid denial by clearly communicating the current reality.*

- **I don't trust you.**
  People will resist change, even if it's good, if trust is lacking between the person initiating the change and themselves.

  *Help: Maintain a solid relationship with them and avoid situations that would lead to misunderstandings or lack of trust.*

CAUTION: When dealing with resistance to change, the best question to ask yourself is:

## CAN I LIVE WITH THIS?

If you can, move on and stop wasting your energy resisting. If you can't, take action to deal with the situation.

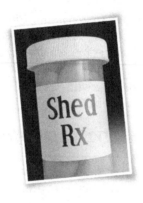

# Embrace Change!
# Resisting just makes it
# more painful.

# SHED MANAGEMENT

# Awareness Management

We are creatures of habit. A study published in the Journal of Abnormal Psychology found that 95% percent of our behaviors occur automatically, unconsciously, or in reaction to an external demand. Only 5% of our actions are consciously selected.

See how you do on the following awareness test.

---

First read the sentence enclosed in the box.

> FINISHED FILES ARE THE RE-
> SULT OF YEARS OF SCIENTIF-
> IC STUDY COMBINED WITH THE
> EXPERIENCE OF MANY YEARS.

Now count the F's in the sentence. Count them only once and do not go back and count them again.

---

There are six F's in the sentence. The average person finds three. Many people do not see the Fs in the word "of".

Sometimes, even though something is right in front of us, we lack awareness. We're usually operating on autopilot. Only when our awareness is heightened, can we consciously take action and make better choices that promote growth.

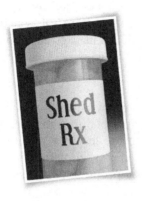

Heighten your awareness. It is the key in any behavior change.

# Energy Management

Managing energy is critical for sustainable success - for ourselves, our organizations, our environment. Some experts say it's "all about energy" and it's the single most important issue facing our survival as a civilization. Now we might not be able to manage the global energy crisis, but we *can* learn to be more personally energy efficient.

**Stop the Leak**
If Eckert Tolle is anywhere close to being right with his statistic that 93% of our thoughts are repetitive and useless, then: stop the leak! We are wasting the large majority of our energy. Topping the list of energy siphoners are toxic people and negative thinking. Avoid these at all cost.

**Energy Management**

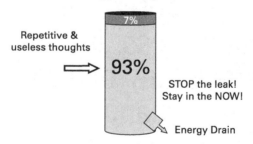

Repetitive & useless thoughts

7%

93%

STOP the leak!
Stay in the NOW!

Energy Drain

**Stay Above the Acceptance Line**
All emotional responses emit energy. Positive, or "Wahoo!", responses, create energy. Negative, or "Oh, no!", responses

drain energy. Acceptance is a neutral zone that will neither emit or drain energy. Managing your emotional responses to situations will help you manage your energy most efficiently.

You might find it difficult to say, "Wahoo!" to everything that happens to you. Instead, make a goal of keeping your energy at the neutral zone of acceptance or higher.

### Energy Management Zones

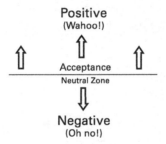

**Manage your energy, not your time**
We are being asked to do more, and more, and more with less and less and less. *Harvard Business Review* published an article by Tony Schwartz, author of *"The Way We're Working Isn't Working."*

In the article, Schwartz claims the new skill for future success will be, "manage your energy, not your time." He encourages people to foster simple rituals that help replenish physical, emotional and mental resilience.

These include taking brief breaks at specific intervals, expressing appreciation to others, reducing interruptions, and spending more time on activities you enjoy most and do best. Healthcare workers counsel consumers toward healthier eating, sleeping and exercise habits, but many of them don't heed their own advice. What are the first things that we end up shedding that we *shouldn't* shed when work demands increase? Eating, sleeping, exercise.

Increased work demands require more energy and a faster refueling capacity. When was the last time you did an energy audit on yourself?

Take a few moments and conduct a personal energy audit now. Use the chart below to list what gives you energy and what drains it.

### Energy Audit

| Gives you energy | Drains your energy |
|---|---|
|  |  |
|  |  |
|  |  |
|  |  |
|  |  |

**Recharge every 90 minutes**
Ernest Rossi's entire book, *The 20 Minute Break*, focuses on our "Ultradian" cycle. This is the body's need for regular

recharge. Every 90 minutes to two hours we experience more focused attention followed by a 20-minute period of lesser focus. During the 20-minute recharge, the body is restoring energy.

Basically, we continue to oscillate all day from a higher to lower level of arousal and alertness.

### Our Body's Ultradian Cycle

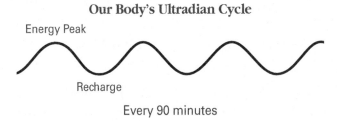

Energy Peak

Recharge

Every 90 minutes

The following are the body's signs it is time to recharge:
- Restless, wanting to stretch and move
- Yawning and sighing
- Wanting a snack
- The call of nature
- The inability to concentrate as well as before
- The inability to "find the right word"

Most of us, lured by work demands and tightly organized schedules, habitually ignore these signs and override the body's need to recharge.

This is when many people grab a candy bar, a cigarette or a cup of coffee as a way to "cheat" their bodies' cry for a break and keep plowing through the day.

Especially in healthcare, we often regard resting as a weakness, a waste of time or a major inconvenience. I distinctly remember my early years in the ER when the longer you could stay in the trauma room without a break of any kind, the better nurse you were. Talk about bladder control! On crazy days when the hospital was on "divert status," there was no one to relieve us. Like a soldier on the battlefield, we'd be stuck for eight hours with no water or bathroom breaks.

You might get away with ignoring your body for a while, but sooner or later, it will cost you.

It's like trying to defibrillate a patient who has gone into cardiac arrest and someone forgot to recharge the machine. (Unfortunately, that actually happens.)

So, don't you think it makes sense to work with your body's natural flow and not against it?

Recharge Reminders:
- Don't ignore the warning signs your body is giving you
- Take a break every 90 minutes to two hours
- Learn how to set limits and keep healthy boundaries. It's OK to say "no!"
- Take advantage of your natural peaks and valleys
- Know when you are running at your top efficiency mode for work productivity

In workplaces where regular breaks are encouraged, productivity increases and rates of sickness decrease.

## 40 Instant Energy Boosters

These energy boosters take five minutes or less and you can do all of them at work.

1. Go for a walk
2. Laugh
3. Eat a healthy power snack
4. Have a mint
5. Hug someone
6. Get some sunlight
7. Meditate
8. Smile
9. Massage your eyes and temples
10. Text someone that you're thinking about them
11. Sing your favorite song
12. Change chairs
13. Drink water
14. Have a piece of chocolate
15. Splash some water on your face
16. Have a cup of tea
17. Change your shoes
18. Stand up and stretch
19. Tell a joke
20. Take 2-3 deep cleansing breaths
21. Make a grateful list
22. Give a compliment
23. Sniff citrus or lavender
24. Do 10 jumping jacks
25. Eat some yogurt
26. Give yourself a mini massage

27. Stomp your feet 10 times
28. List what you've accomplished
29. Engage in a random act of kindness
30. Put on a bright accessory
31. Roll up and down on your toes
32. Grab a handful of nuts
33. Munch on some berries
34. Rub your hands together
35. Hug yourself
36. Engage with a positive person
37. Write an encouraging note
38. Take a restroom break
39. Use self-acupressure — squeeze your thumb
40. Look in the mirror and tell yourself how awesome you are!

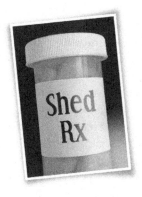

# Take a recharge break every 90 minutes!

# Control Management

One of the biggest challenges people encounter with change goes back to the familiar serenity prayer.

> *Grant me the serenity to accept the things I cannot change; courage to change the things I can; and wisdom to know the difference.*

Control varies with each situation we experience. Identifying what situations we actually have control of will be help us manage change and our energy most effectively. On one end of the scale we have full control. On the other end, we have no control. Somewhere in the middle we have some influence over a situation.

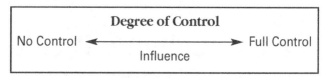

The goal is to clearly understand where the degree of control is in each situation. Evaluate whether you have:

1. No Control
2. Influence
3. Control

The following control chart gives a few examples of possible challenging work situations. Depending upon your role, you may identify different areas of no control, influence and control.

## Control Chart

| Situation | No Control | Influence | Control |
|---|---|---|---|
| Healthcare reform | Implementation of federal policy | Counseling others about their health | Personal healthcare and lifestyle habits |
| Negative co-worker | Their attitude and behavior | Amount of time spent around them | Your attitude and behavior |
| Electronic Medical Record | Choosing the system | Suggestions for revisions | When to sign up for training class |

Taking time to clearly identify where your control actually lies will help you navigate change more effectively.

Where do most of us waste our energy? On the things we have no control over. Make a conscious effort to not let control issues rob you of your precious time and energy. Strive to focus on all the things you have control over today!

## 25 Things You Can Control NOW

1. How much you worry about things you can't control
2. How many positive vs. negative thoughts you have
3. How hard you work
4. How often you judge others
5. The number of times you smile and say thank you
6. How much time you spend in the present moment, the NOW
7. How quickly you respond to others
8. How you deal with anger
9. How much you express concern and compassion for others
10. The friends that you surround yourself with
11. How you interpret situations that occur
12. How quickly you get back up after disappointment or failure
13. How you communicate to others
14. How you express your feelings
15. How prepared and organized you are
16. How well you listen
17. The amount and type of food you ingest
18. How much sleep you get
19. How much you exercise
20. What you read and watch on TV
21. How grateful and appreciative you are
22. How well you treat yourself
23. How quickly you release your emotional attachments
24. How quickly you reframe the situation
25. How quickly you refocus your energy

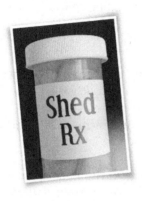

Focus your energy
on things you can
control or influence.

# Personal Shedding

Shedding is not always easy, but it is not as difficult as we make it. It is 100% your choice! Here are some practical shedding tips for stopping unhealthy behaviors.

**S** top and reflect!

**H** onestly identify what behavior you want to SHED or stop doing. Set a realistic goal.

**E** stablish a support system - healthy friends, a counselor or support group.

**D** etermine what environmental factors trigger the undesired behavior. Then avoid them!

**D** istract yourself by discovering two positive addictions such as exercise, journaling, meditation or gardening.

**I** dentify someone to be your accountability partner and call them when you feel triggered.

**N** ever beat yourself up. Learn from your mistakes! Reward yourself for small, incremental successes.

**G** ive yourself positive daily affirmations - say them 15 times a day. Place them everywhere – on mirrors, refrigerators, car dashboards and doors.

***Ready, Set, SHED!***

# To SHED or Not to SHED?

One of the most frequently asked questions I get when I speak around the country is, "How do I know when to SHED?" Given all the various circumstances we each face, the answer to that question can be extremely challenging. Here are five filter questions that will help you determine if it is time to SHED.

1. **Is the situation causing suffering for the organization, others or me?** Pain is a warning sign, an alarm that something is wrong. If the organization or someone within it is suffering, it may be time to SHED.

2. **Will shedding promote health and growth for the organization, others or me?** What growth might occur? It may be painful at first but similar to pruning a bush, shedding often promotes accelerated growth.

3. **What fears are involved?** If someone is over attached, there is usually a core fear that needs to be identified and dealt with.

4. **What are the benefits of shedding for the organization, others or me?** List all possible advantages both long and short term.

5. **What consequences will occur if I don't SHED?** No decision is actually making a decision not to SHED and there usually is a price to pay. Identify what might be the repercussions if nothing is done?

# Avoiding the Three Deadly Syndromes

## COPD

What does COPD stand for? Being in healthcare you might say Chronic Obstructive Pulmonary Disease. Well, 99.9% of the time you would be correct. But with respect to shedding, COPD stands for:

**C** hronic

**O** pposition to

**P** roperly

**D** etach

It afflicts those who continue to resist change and won't shed. Not being able to detach is a form of a breathing disorder. When people get afraid or anxious what is the first thing they stop doing?

Breathing.

What happens if you hold your breath? You will eventually pass out or die. Just as breathing oxygen in and $CO_2$ out is part of our body's way of sustaining life, so is attachment and detachment. If we don't properly detach, we will hold on to $CO_2$ toxins that will eventually cause us harm and restrict our ability to live.

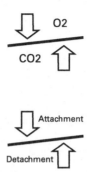

We need to regularly assess our ability to fully breathe and experience all of life's attachments and detachments, just like we regularly assess post operative and COPD patients with an incentive spirometer, the medical device that measures the volume of air exhaled from the lungs.

Treatment: Actively take steps to strengthen your shedding lungs. Resuscitate yourself if needed. Commit to yourself that no matter what happens you will keep moving forward by fully inhaling and exhaling through the challenging situation.

# Above the Neck Constipation!

Above the Neck Constipation is the result of "stinking thinking" - the negative thinking that has a tendency to consume us.

Complaining leads the constipation pack. It's a downward spiral from there. Ever work with someone who just drains your energy with their negatively? You can feel it when they walk in the room. Negativity, like an infectious virus, siphons precious energy and productivity.

Sometimes negative thinking stems from deep roots. It may be something somebody said to you 30 years ago and you keep playing it over and over again in your head. *"I am not good enough, smart enough or rich enough."* We create what we think about and we become the people we hang around. Be careful: Above the Neck Constipation can cause a huge system blockage.

Treatment: A mental enema!

Here are 5 ways to SHED negativity, together they constitute the mental enema formula.

1. SHED complaining
2. Avoid toxic people
3. Stop playing negative mental tapes
4. Focus on the positive and what's right
5. Remind yourself: The GAS will PASS!

*You either SHED or get off the pot!*

# Vitamin "B" Deficiency

Vitamin B deficiency isn't the medical syndrome most of us are familiar with — it is the lack of being. Our society values doing. We are hired at our jobs to get things done. The question is not should I "be" or should I "do", but to "be" while you are doing.

Have you ever been talking with someone and then, all of the sudden, you realize you have no idea what they just said to you? It's embarrassing, isn't it? We all do it.

When we are at work, we are thinking about all the things we need to do at home. When we are at home, we are thinking about all the things we need to do at work and we are never where we are.

A staggering 80% of all accidents occur because people are not in the now - they are suffering from Vitamin B deficiency. They are multi-tasking, distracted or their brains have gone to Aruba. A recent Harvard Business Review article by Peter Bergman says that multitasking leads to as much as a 40% drop in productivity, increased stress, and a 10% drop in IQ.

Vitamin B deficiency is hitting epidemic levels. Stop and take an assessment of your own habits. Ignoring the signs and symptoms of Vitamin B deficiency will ultimately cause damage to your work productively and personal relationships.

Treatment: Wherever you are, BE there!

# SURVIVAL GUIDE: SHED OR YOU'RE DEAD

# SHED STYLES

# Development of the SHED Style™ Model

For centuries, people have sought to find a systematic way to understand human behavior and to explain the differences in others. Our expanded comprehension of psychology and advances in research has led to an evolution of different models based on concepts dating back to Hippocrates in 450 B.C. Interestingly, many models have one common characteristic: they group behaviors into four categories.

So, in 2007, when I developed the SHED Style Model, I created it with four categories as well. It was based on the powerful metaphor of shedding. It was concise and a quick learn and people immediately knew what the words Stabilizer, Hedger, Energizer and Driver meant - SHED! The tool does not depend on a long assessment or lengthy report.

The tool's primary focus is to provide practical strategies on how to effectively lead and manage rapid change. The goal in utilizing this tool in the workplace is to engage employees, reduce negativity, and increase productivity and bottom line results.

The power of any assessment tool is increased awareness. This is the critical first step in making positive changes at work and life. Most successful people know themselves well, recognize their strengths and know their opportunities for growth. They are experts at adapting their behaviors in order to achieve positive results.

# Understanding Your SHED Style

Use this exercise to determine your SHED style.

### Shed Style Assessment Tool

Work across the page. Number the words in each row. Give 4 to the word that best describes you, 3 to next, then 2, and then a 1 to the least. Your first response is probably the best. Scoring: Add up each column. Put totals inside the shapes on the bottom.

| | | | |
|---|---|---|---|
| ☐ Feelings | ☐ Details | ☐ Possibilities | ☐ Facts |
| ☐ Security | ☐ Order | ☐ Inspiration | ☐ Control |
| ☐ Patient | ☐ Accurate | ☐ Talkative | ☐ Bold |
| ☐ Cooperative | ☐ Analytical | ☐ Enthusiastic | ☐ Competitive |
| ☐ Loyal | ☐ Reserved | ☐ Optimistic | ☐ Daring |
| ☐ Agreement | ☐ Quality | ☐ Ideas | ☐ Results |
| ☐ Calm | ☐ Logical | ☐ Persuasive | ☐ Driven |
| ◯ | ☐ | ◯ | △ |

Now transfer your scores by plotting them to the graph on the next page Then draw a line from each score to create a bar graph.

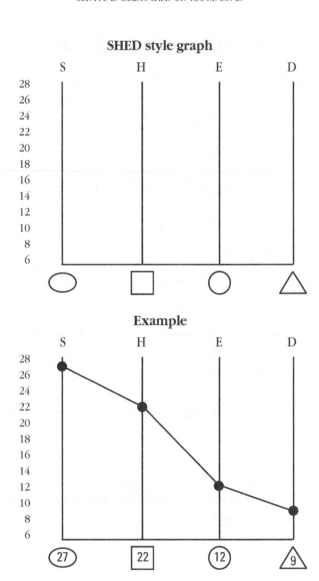

**SHED style graph**

**Example**

There are four SHED styles. Each of us comprises a mixture of ALL four but most of us have a primary and secondary preference.

1. Identify what your primary and secondary score.
2. Read the summary of the four styles below.
3. Highlight the 2-3 things that really resonate to you.

**Stabilizer**
Stabilizers create a stable and harmonious work environment. They provide caring and consistency. Their focus is on cooperating with others to get the job done. They demonstrate patience and are extremely good listeners.

**Hedger**
Hedgers create order and bring a systematic approach to the work environment. They provide quality and accuracy. They excel in finding logical solutions. They demonstrate attention to detail, and weigh out the cons and pros.

**Energizer**
Energizers create life and inspire others in the work environment. They look at the positive side and the unlimited possibilities. They demonstrate enthusiasm and a fun-loving desire to connect with people.

**Driver**
Drivers create results in the work environment. They provide action, set goals and quickly move towards accomplishing them. They take control of situations, solve problems and accept multiple challenges.

# Adapting Your SHED Style to Achieve Positive Results

Everyone has a preferred style in which they behave and communicate with others. However, very few people realize:

*We are 75% less effective when we don't adapt our style in response to others.*

Let's look at the four styles to see how you might adapt your style to achieve positive results.

**Stabilizers,** of all the styles, dislike change the most. In fact if you were 100% a stabilizer, you would hate change. When you think about it, it makes perfect sense because the stabilizers' strength is to stabilize. If you are dealing with a stabilizer with regards to change, give them as much notice as possible. If you are going to change their shift, tell them now if it will be in January of 2026!

**Hedgers** are into data and details. When change happens, they ask one question over and over and over again: Why? Why? Why? If you are dealing a hedger with regards to change, come with data, information and a contract signed by the attorney. Allow hedgers to play devil's advocate. They often think about the details that everyone else overlooks.

**Energizers** get excited about change. In fact some don't even care what the change is they are so excited about the possibilities. They just want to throw a party and celebrate. If you are dealing with change, get the energizers on board *first*. If you do, the excitement will be contagious!

**Drivers** drive change. They make things happen. They do have a theme song with regards to change. Remember Frank Sinatra's famous song, "My Way"? If you want change to be successful, get Drivers involved. You might even consider figuring out how you can make it more of their idea.

The SHED Style Summary gives an overview of each style's strengths and challenges and a few change communication strategies to consider using.

## SHED Style Summary

| Styles | Strengths | Challenges | Change Communication Strategies |
|---|---|---|---|
| **S**tabilizer | Stability<br>Good listeners<br>Team players | Dislikes sudden change | • Approach slowly, don't demand.<br>• Provide as much reassurance of stability and what won't change as is available.<br>• Give as much notice of change as possible.<br>• Acknowledge feelings and offer support. |
| **H**edger | Order<br>Quality<br>Accuracy | Analysis paralysis | • Give logic and provide lots of information<br>• Address 'why' the change is going to occur.<br>• Demonstrate how change will improve quality.<br>• Allow them to play devil's advocate and address something possibly overlooked. |
| **E**nergizer | Positive<br>Fun people<br>Unlimited possibilities | Working alone, Details | • Be enthusiastic about the change.<br>• Help them get excited about the possibilities.<br>• Focus on how change will improve approval from others.<br>• Engage them and they will become the cheerleaders for change efforts! |
| **D**river | Results<br>Action orientated<br>Quick | Being controlled by others | • Get to point quickly.<br>• Give options and allow them to be part of change decision if possible.<br>• Explain what's currently wrong and needs change.<br>• Focus on efficiency and results. |

Think of situation at work or someone who drives you crazy. You may think at times that their mission in life is to make your life hell.

Consider that maybe they are just operating from another SHED style. Many conflicts are due to the inability to adapt to the extreme opposite style with regards to PACE of CHANGE and INFORMATIONAL NEEDS. The further apart you are on these scales, the more you will need to adapt to the other person's style.

For example, when looking at the pace of change, the Driver and the Stabilizer are on opposite extremes. Because the pace of change is the fastest with Drivers, they often demand change from others in a more abrupt manner. So instead of the Driver demanding that the Stabilizer, "Just do it now because I said so!" the Driver could slow down and approach the Stabilizer by listening and providing additional data and information about *why* the change is taking place. Ironically, this delivers results quicker in the long run.

On the other hand, if you are approaching a Driver, pick up the pace and get to the point quickly!

## Adapting your pace and information needs

**Pace of Change**

| | |
|---|---|
| Stabilizer | Slower |
| Hedger | |
| Energizer | |
| Driver | Faster |

**Information Needs**

| | |
|---|---|
| Energizer | Less Details |
| Driver | |
| Stabilizer | |
| Hedger | More Details |

**CAUTION:** Adaptation goes way beyond the initial awareness of taking assessment tools. It requires a daily commitment to adapt behaviors to achieve positive results.

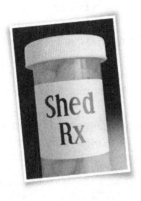

Adapting your
SHED style will
make you 75% more
effective.

# How to Lead a More Efficient Team

### *How do you spell SHED?*

### **S-H-E-D**

If one letter is missing, you can't spell SHED.

And if one style is missing or not significantly represented, your team may not be running as effectively as possible.

All SHED styles play an important role in an organization. See what happens to an organization if a SHED style is not represented or if everyone is the same SHED style.

| Style | If nobody was... | If everybody was... |
|---|---|---|
| Stabilizer | Chaos, no stability | Change doesn't happen, too stable, status quo |
| Hedger | No organization, wouldn't pass JCAHO survey | Analysis paralysis |
| Energizer | Dull, boring, low morale | Party!!! |
| Driver | Needed change efforts fail | Intense conflict and fighting |

All four SHED styles bring something critical and significant to the team.

Stabilizer ⟶ Brings stability

Hedger ⟶ Brings order

Energizer ⟶ Brings enthusiasm

Driver ⟶ Brings results

CAUTION: Any strength overdeveloped or stressed can become your weakness.

### What happens when you're stressed or you overdevelop your style?

Stabilizers become hesitant and overly sensitive.

Hedgers become critical and overly focused.

Energizers become distracted and overly flexible.

Drivers can become blunt and overly demanding.

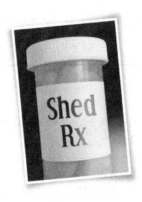

All four SHED styles
must be represented to
run an efficient team.

# SHED LEADERSHIP

# How to Help Other People SHED?

### *Five Proven Strategies to*
### *Seize the Power of Change*

According to Gallup Poll's calculations, actively disengaged employees cost the American economy up to $350 billion a year in lost productivity.

Disengaged employees are those who refuse to SHED. Their negativity and resistance to change can cripple an organization. For a workforce to be at peak productivity, it needs everyone to be in Super-shedder mode. Following are five proven strategies that can help you and your team to seize the power of change.

1. **Attach to something new.** Humans have a natural tendency to attach to familiar people, processes and products. Remember when you were a child and someone took away your lollipop? You probably screamed and cried and thought your life as a four-year-old had come to an end. Minutes later, in the heat of your temper tantrum, someone handed you a cuddly teddy bear and immediately your eyes lit up and the crying halted. The lollipop? Who cared? Life was good now that you were attached to the teddy bear!

   This strategy also works in the workplace. How can you help others get excited about the change (the cuddly new teddy bear) so shedding the attachment to the familiar (the lollipop) can occur faster? Watch resistance to change magically evaporate as you uncover ways for your team to attach to something new.

2. **Shrink the change.** Dan and Chip Heath discuss shrinking the change in their book, *Switch: How to Change Things When Change is Hard.* Too fast or too big of a change will overwhelm and paralyze a workforce. If a proposed change is perceived as insurmountable, people will shut down and give up before you even get out of the gate. So shrink change down to bite-size, easily digestible pieces by providing a more achievable goal. If your target is to improve productivity by 50% this year, consider the more realistic goal of 5% monthly. To keep peak motivation, don't forget to publically recognize and celebrate short term wins! Momentum is vital for sustainable results.

3. **Give the goal with choices.** My mom was not in executive leadership but she knew the value of the "goal with choices" strategy extremely well. Her goal: A clean house. What were my choices? "Kathy, do you want to take out the trash or do the dishes?" I didn't want to do either, but somehow I was more motivated because I had a choice of household chores. Likewise, employees' motivation soars if they're given more control over a situation. Peter Bragman, from *Harvard Business Review*, offers another slant on this tip. Give the desired outcome, and then suggest the path. Allow people to reject the path as long as they chose an alternate route to the same destination.

4. **Eliminate the fear.** While working at a healthcare system years ago, the CEO announced to all 4,000 employees that they were going through tremendous change. He said that anyone who came up with an innovative idea to save time or money — even if it changed or eliminated their job — would have a place to work somewhere in the system. What a brilliant idea! The CEO eliminated the employees' fear of losing their jobs. You might not be able to guarantee 100% job security, consider how you can build strategies that eliminate as much fear as possible.

5. **Create a sense of urgency.** The dictionary defines urgency as: "something that compels immediate action or attention." John Kotter, the change guru, claims, "Without an organization-wide sense of urgency, it's like trying to build a pyramid on a foundation of empty shoeboxes."

How are you creating a sense of urgency with your employees? Spark the motivation for change with open and honest communication. Talk about what's happening in your industry and with your competition. Discuss the trends, the facts and the consequences for team members and the organization if change doesn't occur. Without cooperation or buy-in, your change efforts will fail. By stimulating people to talk and think, you'll propel them to move out of denial or anger. Urgency provides the fire to ignite teams to get on board with the exciting possibilities.

# 7 New Skills
# Every Healthcare Worker Needs

Below are seven new skills every healthcare worker needs, as well as a few suggestions on how to build the specific skill in your team members.

## 1. Learning on the fly
- Set a new expectation: "What we are hiring you for today, is probably not what we are going to ask you to do tomorrow."
- Encourage people to embrace temporary as the new norm.
- Eliminate language such as, "That is the way we have always done it."

## 2. Reframing
- Describe a situation where you observed someone's inability to reframe. What were the consequences?
- Identify past successes of your reframe-ability.
- Play the "Reframe Game" – list challenges and see who can come up with the best reframe.

## 3. Refocusing
- Be in the now!
- SHED multi-tasking and identify ways to minimize distractions.
- Ready, Set, SHED! Set a timer and a goal. Reward yourself when you're done.

## 4. Energy management
- Conduct an energy audit.
- Describe your typical day.
- Establish healthy rituals to replenish your energy.

## 5. Adaptive style
- Be aware of your preferred SHED style.
- Learn how to quickly read other people's SHED style.
- Identify one change strategy to adapt your SHED style.

## 6. Curiosity
- Embrace philosopher Marshall McLuhan's mindset: "If it works, it's obsolete."
- Engage your team in a "What if" exploration exercise. (Example: What if there was no wait time in the ER?)
- Play the "Innovation Game" - Take an object and in three minutes identify as many uses other than the original use.

## 7. Certain uncertainty
- Schedule a "Panic Now" Party - Give your team a dire situation, like a computer system crash, and ask them what they would do.
- Play "Fear Factor" - List your organization's current challenges and ask employees about their biggest fears surrounding those challenges.
- SHED worry. Take action. Keep moving forward despite fear!

# Who Killed Communication?

**Shedding the top 10 communication killers**

Poor communication can have dire consequences. Back in the mid 90's, I was the administrator on-call for a hospital when I received a disturbing phone call from the house supervisor. She said, "A patient just came out of surgery for a left leg amputation, but somehow we cut off the wrong leg!"

Chills went through my body. How could this be? The surgery staff did everything correctly but they overlooked one thing. A miscommunication of one little word, "right" verses "left," caused this tragic outcome. Every day, communication is killed. And when this happens, there is always a price to pay; lost revenue, decreased productivity, low morale or top talent that flees. In healthcare, miscommunication can lead to serious medical errors or even to death. Nobody can afford the cost of miscommunication in healthcare. The crime is often committed unintentionally but the punishment can be astronomical.

**Here are the top 10 communication killers.**

1. **Not focusing on the outcomes.** Most people start communicating and never stop to ask what outcomes they want. What do you want people to know, feel, and do different as a result of the communication? Diving deeper into how you want people to feel and do can dramatically change the outcomes and how you communicate.

2. **Not listening.** Listening is the least taught skill growing up in school, yet it is the most important skill after you graduate. Most people do not practice active listening and aren't paying attention when someone is talking. They are busy thinking about their response. Understand that people want to feel heard more than they care about whether you agree with them.

3. **Not addressing WIIFM.** People want to know: WIIFM - or "what's in it for me?" Whether people verbalize it or not, everyone at some level is focused on how a situation is going to affect them. To communicate most effectively and get the results you desire, take a moment to look at the situation from the other person's perspective.

4. **Not getting feedback.** Just assuming you understand what is being said can be dangerous. Always summarize the conversation and ask for clarification. Ask, "What did you hear me say?"

5. **Not agreeing on next steps.** Who is doing what, and when? Don't forget to obtain consensus with next steps and a timeline. Be open to possibilities and give people as many choices as possible. Especially when people are communicating about something they might not want to do, choices give people a sense of empowerment.

6. **Not following through or holding people accountable.** Clearly communicating accountability

expectations for yourself and others is key. Are you following through with what you committed to do? Are you holding other people accountable for what they have agreed to do? Using this simple NET guideline will help:

What are the needs?

What are the expectations?

What is the time frame?

7. **Not using the most effective communication tool.** Many people default to one or two communication tools – face to face, phone calls, emails, text messages – and overuse them for most of their communication whether the tool works best or not. All of the tools have advantages and disadvantages. Sometimes you need to use multiple tools. For example, after a face-to-face meeting, which lacks documentation, follow up with an email summarizing what you understood and the agreement on the next steps.

8. **Not choosing the right time.** You can have the right message but if it's delivered at the wrong time, it can lead to disastrous results. Remember, timing is everything!

9. **Being judgmental.** Jumping to conclusions is very easy to do, especially when people have their own biased mental models of how things should be. Respond, don't react. A few phrases to avoid are: "You always…" and "You never…" These words elicit defensiveness in others. Using words and phrases such

as: "Help me understand...", "I am confused...", "When I see...", "I feel..." or "I've noticed..." help create a climate of trust and openness.

10. **Not acknowledging and rewarding good communication.** Don't forget to stop and celebrate communication success. Ken Blanchard, author of The One Minute Manager, says, "Catch people doing things right!"

Remember the mystery of *Who Killed Communication* is easily solved. **Miss Communication** always is the culprit!

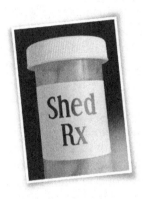

# Before communicating ask yourself:

1. Is it true?
2. Does it need to be said?
3. Is it likely the person will respond to me?

# 35 Strategies
# to Keep Communication Alive!

1. Identify your outcomes before your start
2. Address WIIFM for all involved
3. Look for common ground instead of differences
4. Identify and involve major stakeholders
5. Acknowledge changes that may be difficult or inconvenient
6. Ask for clarification of what was heard
7. Obtain consensus with an action plan, and establish next steps with a timeline
8. Follow through with your commitments
9. Follow up with other people's commitments
10. Give your undivided attention to those who you are communicating with - practice active listening
11. Make time to communicate
12. Choose the best method to communicate
13. Ask for feedback — "What's working? What's not?"
14. Create a climate of trust and openness
15. Keep a positive attitude
16. Respond, don't react
17. Be open to possibilities
18. Acknowledge your own mental models
19. Set clear expectations
20. Identify when to communicate - timing is everything!
21. Discuss how disagreements are to be handled
22. Be honest with yourself and others
23. Understand that people want to feel heard more than they care about whether you agree with them
24. Discuss communication barriers

25. Encourage participation
26. Utilize your resources
27. Acknowledge fears
28. Decide what information should be available and when
29. Over communicate when change is significant
30. Give people as many choices as possible
31. Use good non-verbal skills including eye contact, body language and voice inflection
32. Be non-judgmental
33. Conduct a communication audit
34. Acknowledge and reward good communication. Celebrate success!
35. Adjust your SHED style to get positive results

# Ready, Set, SHED!

# Avoiding Premature Death

Nobody is getting out of this life alive. We all are going to die. However, we can avoid dying *before* our time.

As I reflect back on my own life, I almost needlessly caused my own premature death in 1987.

After working in the ER and being exposed to a trauma victim who had AIDS, I found myself carrying the unwanted title of the first healthcare worker in America to test positive from a workplace exposure.

I didn't cope with the diagnosis well. I stopped eating, sleeping and exercising. My negative thoughts were consuming me. I eventually found myself in a hotel parking lot with a bottle of pills in my hand.

If it hadn't of been for someone who knocked on my car window, I would have been dead.

Inexplicably, three months later all of my test results returned negative. I didn't have AIDS after all.

This life transforming "wake-up call" clearly revealed one of my serious flaws: I didn't have the skills to cope with change. Basically, I didn't know how to SHED.

Nobody knows what life will hand them. But we *do* have 100% control over our response to life's twists and turns and we can equip ourselves with the knowledge and skills to navigate professional and personal changes.

Life is change. Growth is optional.

Chose wisely!

SHED or YOU'RE DEAD!

CAUTION: Life is challenging. We all need support. As Dr. John Bolinger would often tell me in treatment team meetings at the hospital: "People can handle just about anything if they have three things: honesty, a plan and support."

# Lenny's Favorite Quotes to SHED for Success™

1. People don't resist change. They resist being changed! — *Peter Senge*

2. It's not the strongest of the species that survive, nor the most intelligent, but the ones most responsive to change. — *Charles Darwin*

3. The problem is never how to get new, innovative thoughts into your mind, but how to get the old ones out. — *Dee Hock*

4. To obtain knowledge, add things every day. To obtain wisdom, subtract things everyday. — *Lao Tsu*

5. If it works, it's obsolete. — *Marshall McLuhan*

6. Change is hard because people overestimate the value of what they have—and underestimate the value of what they may gain by giving that up. — *Flight of the Buffalo*

7. Some people change when they see the light, others when they feel the heat. — *Caroline Schoeder*

8. The future belongs to those who see possibilities before they become obvious. — *John Scully*

9. If you want to truly understand something, try to change it. — *Kurt Lewin*

10. Holding on to anger is like grasping a hot coal with the intent of throwing it at someone else; you are the one who gets burned. — *Buddha*

11. Know thyself… — *Socrates*

12. The greatest danger in times of turbulence is not the turbulence; it is to act with yesterday's logic. — *Peter Drucker*

13. Your success in life isn't based on your ability to simply change. It is based on your ability to change faster than your competition, customers and business. — *Mark Sanborn*

14. If I would have asked my customers what they wanted, they would have told me a bigger mule. — *Henry Ford*

15. The first step toward change is awareness. The second step is acceptance. — *Nathaniel Branden*

16. Courage is the power to let go of the familiar. — *Raymond Lindquist*

17. Just when the caterpillar thought it was over, it became a butterfly. — *Unknown*

18. The secret of change is to focus all your energy, not on fighting for the old, but on building the new. — *Socrates*

19. Be the change you wish to see in the world. — *Ghandi*

20. In times of change, those who shed will grow and prosper; those who refuse to shed will find themselves well-equipped for an organization (and life) that no longer exists. — *Eric Hoffer, Philosopher as paraphrased by Lenny the Lizard*

**Happy Shedding!**

# SHED for Success™ Rx Reminders

1. Take care of your body. Where else are you going to live?
2. Embody *temporary* as the norm.
3. Commit to being a Super-shedder!
4. It's 100% your choice: Shed or You're Dead!
5. Routinely ask yourself, what no longer serves me?
6. Learning to navigate life's attachments and detachments is critical to your success and happiness.
7. Practice the 3 R's of Shedding: Release, Reframe, Refocus.
8. If you want to change, change your mental models first!
9. Revisit and adjust your expectations.
10. When change occurs, acknowledge the loss and move towards acceptance.
11. SHEDebrate! The more change, the more you need to celebrate!
12. Courageously embrace your fear and take action!
13. Embrace change! Resisting just makes it more painful.
14. Heighten your awareness. It is the key in any behavior change.
15. Take a recharge break every 90 minutes!
16. Focus your energy on things you can control or influence.
17. Adapting your SHED style will make you 75% more effective.
18. All four SHED styles must be represented to run an efficient team.
19. Before communicating ask yourself: Is it true? Does it need to be said? Is it likely the person will respond to me?
20. SHED! SHED! SHED!

# YOUR SHED PAGE

You finished the book, so now what?

Take some time and list the top ideas you took away from the book in the space below.

# Your Personal SHED Rx Action Plan

Pick the most important concepts from your SHED page and identify what will you shed today.

Start doing:

Stop doing:

Continue doing:

Now SHEDebrate your success!

# Acknowledgments

I would like to acknowledge some incredible people in my life who have helped me SHED! If it wasn't for their continued support, I wouldn't have moved to Arizona and this book wouldn't have been written.

Thanks to: Carol Kivler, Grace Brame, Mary Jesunas, Karen Jett, Fred Melton, Patty Kitching, Bob Danzig, Naomi Rhode, Kirstin Carey, and Carol Fredrickson.

Also, my thanks to Ron Black. Our C4 meeting on November 28, 2008 was providence. Ron has taught me the true value and importance of the word "recharge." He frequently reminds me to "stop and smell the cactus."

Also, I'm so grateful for Karen Gilbert, my marketing director, who is a living example of someone who truly believes in the power of shedding and its ability to change lives. She is a daily inspiration to me of someone who keeps shedding despite whatever life throws at you.

A special thanks to Chris Clarke-Epstein, my mentor and "book slave master." Every time I got stuck writing, I could hear her voice all the way from Wisconsin haunting me, "Talking about writing is not writing, writing is writing."

And last, but not least, to my dear friend John Reddish who lost his battle to cancer in 2010. His support, wise advice and sense of humor will be greatly missed.

# About Kathy B. Dempsey

Best known for her creative, unique and innovative approach, Kathy's presentations are engaging, highly interactive and packed full of content for immediate implementation.

Kathy is President of KeepShedding! Inc., a company that ignites organizations with the practical skills and motivation to lead and master change.

Her most popular book, *Shed or You're Dead®: 31 Unconventional Strategies for Change and Growth* is the recipient of a Writer's Digest International Book Award. Kathy is also a contributing author for two of the best-selling *Chicken Soup for the Soul* series.

As a former hospital executive, Kathy led Memorial Health Care System's organizational development efforts to become one of the top 100 hospitals in America.

The Georgia Speakers Association voted Kathy as the Showcase Speaker of the Year and its Master of Influence Honoree. Bob Pikc's Creative Training Techniques International also named her the Trainer of the Year. Kathy is the Past President of the National Speakers Association, Philadelphia Chapter.

She has achieved the highest earned speaker's designation in the world, the Certified Speaking Professional (CSP).

A few of Kathy's clients/sponsors include: Johnson & Johnson, HealthSouth, John Hopkins, Florida Hospital, Stryker, Bayer, Emergency Nurses Association, Michigan Hospital Association, Wal-Mart, American Express, Verizon Wireless, Delta Air Lines, Disney, GSK, Honeywell and American Heart Association.

Kathy is a R.N. and received her Master's of Education in Psychology from the University of Tennessee. A native of Washington D.C, Kathy now resides in Scottsdale, Arizona.

# About Lenny T. Lizard

Lenny the Lizard met Kathy on July 29, 1998 at Memorial Hospital in Chattanooga, Tennessee. Lenny was the result of a life-changing conversation with a colleague about his pet lizard that died because it didn't shed its skin.

It was an instant partnership and Lenny agreed to be her lifelong companion, alter-ego, business partner and vehicle for helping people SHED!

After years of pleading, Kathy finally agreed to relocate from the East Coast and move to Scottsdale, Arizona to be closer to Lenny's relatives.

Lenny is CEO, Chief Energy Officer, of Keep Shedding! Inc. He earned his Ph.D. in Shedding from the world-renowned Reptile University.

Kathy does the speaking but Lenny imparts the real wisdom. He hopes that whenever you see a lizard, it will instantaneously remind you to Keep Shedding!

Over the past 13 years, Lenny and Kathy have inspired thousands of humans to SHED in places around the world including Europe, Canada, Africa, Mexico and across the United States.

Lenny has literally been perched on the top of the heads of some of the most distinguished CEO and executive leaders from Fortune 500 companies, associations and the healthcare industry. (These pictures make for great blackmail and passive income after the event!) Visit KeepShedding.com and click on "About Lenny" page to see his fun adventures and picture portfolio.

# NEED SUPPORT TO HELP YOU SHED?

Sign up for 60 Seconds of Shedding from Lenny the Lizard, a monthly newsletter that gives you 60 seconds of counsel to SHED old habits and thinking and enable personal, professional and organizational growth.

The decision to SHED is sometimes hard and initially only takes a split second decision. Continuing to SHED, to grow and to change takes commitment, perseverance and the encouragement and support of others.

Sign up by visiting www.KeepShedding.com or sending an email to Lenny@KeepShedding.com and include "subscribe" in the subject line.

**For more books, audio CDs and resources,
visit KeepShedding.com**

# Need a System to SHED for Success?

**Sustainability Program**
Infuse every employee and manager in your organization with the skills and motivation to lead and master change by implementing The SHED for Success Sustainability Program. Contact us today to learn how to harness these powerful tools and deliver results for your organization. Some of the components of the program include:

- Employee training
- Leadership training
- Train the trainer sessions
- Consulting
- SHED for Success kits and more

**Speaking Services**
Get your group energized with the skills and motivation to lead and master change by inviting Kathy Dempsey and Lenny to speak at your event.

Contact us today.

www.KeepShedding.com

1-877-5-SHED-NOW!

**(877-574-3366)**

CPSIA information can be obtained
at www.ICGtesting.com
Printed in the USA
FSOW03n0443110416
18998FS